THEY MAKE THE PERFECT BIRTHDAY GIFT!

BE SURE TO READ **ALL THE BABYMOUSE** BOOKS:

HAPPY BIRTHDAY,
BABYMOUSE

BY JENNIFER L. HOLM & MATTHEW HOLM

RANDOM HOUSE 🏠 NEW YORK

Copyright © 2014 by Jennifer Holm and Matthew Holm

All rights reserved. Published in the United States by Random House Children's Books, a division of Random House LLC, a Penguin Random House Company, New York.

Random House and the colophon are registered trademarks of Random House LLC.

Visit us on the Web!
randomhouse.com/kids
Babymouse.com

Educators and librarians, for a variety of teaching tools, visit us at
RHTeachersLibrarians.com

Library of Congress Cataloging-in-Publication Data
Holm, Jennifer L.
Happy birthday, Babymouse / by Jennifer L. Holm & Matthew Holm. — 1st ed.
   p. cm. — (Babymouse ; #18)
Summary: Babymouse imagines the biggest, most wonderful birthday party ever for herself
and tries to make it happen, but Felicia is planning her own birthday bash for the very same day.
ISBN 978-0-307-93161-0 (trade pbk.) — ISBN 978-0-375-97097-9 (lib. bdg.) — ISBN 978-0-307-97544-7 (ebook)
1. Graphic novels. [1. Graphic novels. 2. Imagination—Fiction. 3. Birthdays—Fiction. 4. Parties—Fiction.
5. Mice—Fiction.] I. Holm, Matthew. II. Title.
PZ7.7.H65Hap 2013 741.5'973—dc23 2012039798

MANUFACTURED IN MALAYSIA   10 9 8 7 6 5 4 3 2   First Edition

TIMES SQUARE.

LET'S GO TO OUR REPORTER ON THE GROUND.

WHAT'S THE FEELING LIKE THERE, GEORGIE?

FROM THE VIEW UP HERE, I'D SAY IT'S BABYMOUSE-TASTIC.

FIVE ... FOUR ... THREE ... TWO ... ONE ...

11

LAST YEAR'S BIRTHDAY PARTY.
TRUMPET!
AAAGHH!
WAAHHH!!
GRUNT!
AAAAGH!
ROARRRR!

THE NEXT DAY.

YOU ARE INVITED TO:
BABYMOUSE'S BIRTHDAY BASH!

WHERE:
BABYMOUSE'S HOUSE

WHEN:
1:00 P.M.
SATURDAY

I'VE ALWAYS WONDERED ABOUT SOMETHING, BABYMOUSE.

WHAT?

HOW OLD ARE YOU?

HUH?

YOU NEVER SAY IN THE BOOKS.

BOOKS? WHAT BOOKS?

MAINTAINING THE MYSTERY, I SEE.

17

THE NEXT MORNING.

MAIL

SO WHO DID YOU INVITE, BABYMOUSE?

JUST A FEW PEOPLE.

MAIL

19

TRIP!

GASP!

WHUMP!

27

BABYMOUSE.

I WON'T BE ABLE TO COME TO YOUR BIRTHDAY PARTY, BABYMOUSE....

OH. ARE YOU GOING TO BE OUT OF TOWN?

MY BIRTHDAY PARTY IS THAT DAY.

BUT YOU CAN COME TO MY PARTY IF YOU WANT TO.

AFTER ALL, EVERYBODY ELSE IS GOING TO BE THERE.

UH, GEORGIE?

SHAKE

SHAKE

REALLY, BABYMOUSE.

TYPICAL.

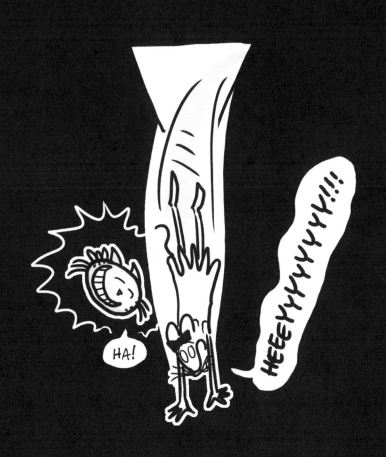

HA!

HEEEYYYYYYY!!!

37

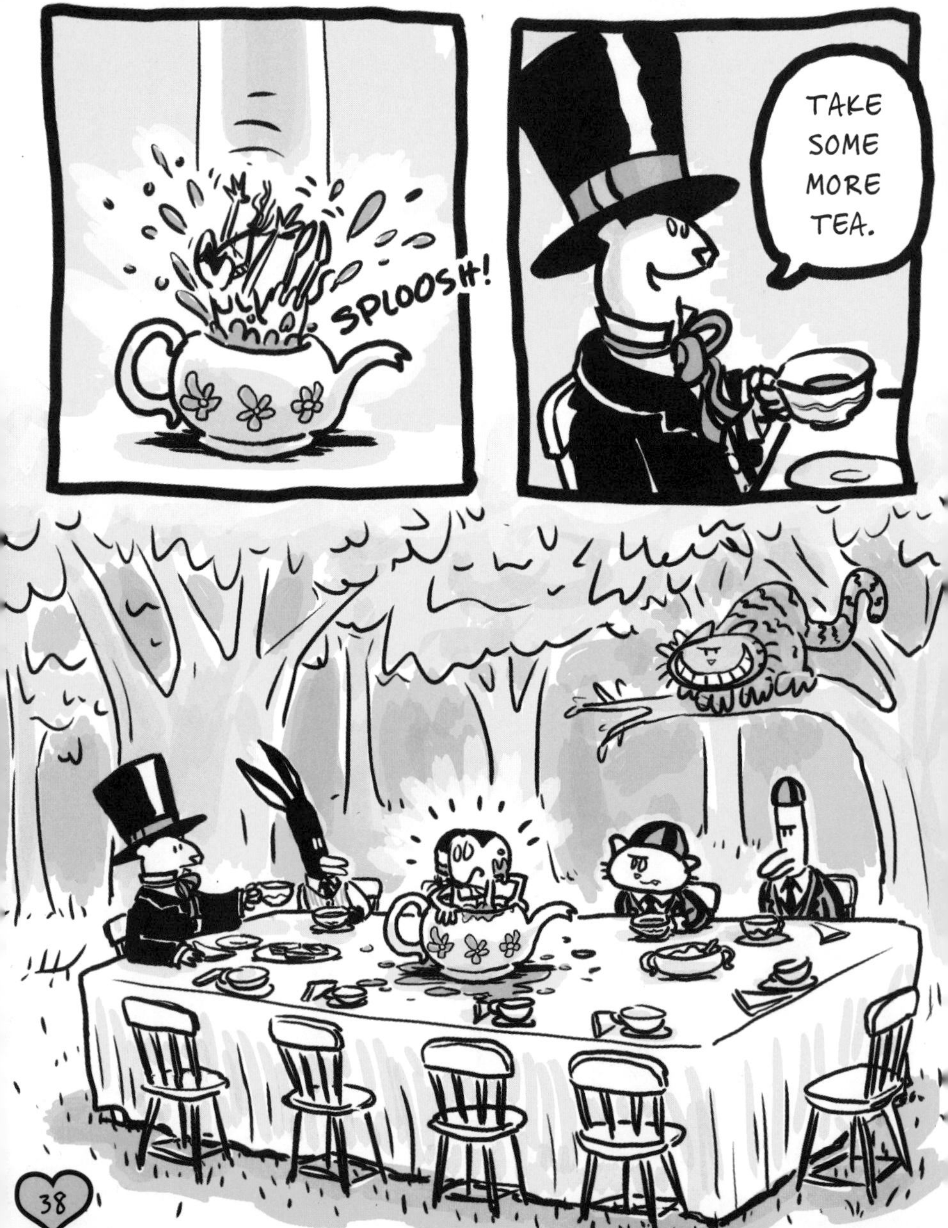
SPLOOSH!
TAKE SOME MORE TEA.

43

THE NEXT DAY.

DING-DONG!

SCREEECH!

CRANK
CREAK

CONTRACT

WELL, IT IS SORT OF A ONE-MAN BAND AND ONE-MONKEY CIRCUS.

TYPICAL.

SCRIBBLE

SCREECH!

45

A FEW DAYS LATER.

CUPCAKES
TAKE THE CAKE

BAKERY

YUM!

WERE YOU LOOKING FOR SOMETHING FOR A SPECIAL OCCASION?

IT'S FOR MY BIRTHDAY PARTY!

GINGERBREAD MEN ARE VERY POPULAR AT BIRTHDAY PARTIES THESE DAYS.

YOU DO KNOW WHAT HAPPENS TO THE GINGERBREAD MAN IN THE ORIGINAL FAIRY TALE, DON'T YOU?

WHAT?

I'LL TAKE THE ONE WITH THE MESSY WHISKERS.

49

THE NEXT DAY.

PETE'S REPTILE AND PIÑATA STORE

THIS THE FURRYPAWS PLACE?

ICE SCULPTURES "R" US

SCREECH!

OOOOH! MY ICE SCULPTURE!

57

A LITTLE LATER.

DING-DONG!

HI! WELCOME TO MY PARTY!

EMU

UH, DO YOU HAVE A BLIMP, TOO?

A BLIMP?

SIGH.

MONDAY AT SCHOOL.
THAT WAS THE BEST BIRTHDAY PARTY EVER!
LOVED THE BLIMP!
THE MILK SHAKE MACHINE WAS GREAT!
AND THE ELEPHANTS WERE FABULOUS!

LOOKS LIKE YOU FINALLY GOT THE PARTY YOU ALWAYS WANTED, HUH, BABYMOUSE?

USA

HAPPY BIRTHDAY, BABYMOUSE!

¡FELIZ CUMPLEAÑOS, BABYMOUSE!

MEXICO

JOYEUX ANNIVERSAIRE, BABYMOUSE!

FRANCE

BABYMOUSE BONUS!

•LEARN HOW TO DRAW THE ALIENS•

BABYMOUSE BONUS!

• FILL IT IN AND MAKE YOUR OWN COMIC •

The search for cupcakes was long.

Even the most faithful cupcake lover lost hope.

Will we _ever_ find cupcakes?

I think I see frosting over the next ridge.

Text by Jenni Holm

GO TO **BABYMOUSE.COM** TO DOWNLOAD A COPY OF THIS PAGE WITH **BLANK** WORD BALLOONS, THEN FILL IT IN WITH YOUR OWN STORY!

If you like Babymouse,
you'll love these other great books
by Jennifer L. Holm!

THE BOSTON JANE TRILOGY
EIGHTH GRADE IS MAKING ME SICK
MIDDLE SCHOOL IS WORSE THAN MEATLOAF
OUR ONLY MAY AMELIA
PENNY FROM HEAVEN
TURTLE IN PARADISE

AND DON'T MISS THE **SQUISH** GRAPHIC NOVELS BY MATTHEW HOLM AND JENNIFER L. HOLM:

#1   SQUISH: Super Amoeba

#2   SQUISH: Brave New Pond

#3   SQUISH: The Power of the Parasite

#4   SQUISH: Captain Disaster

#5   SQUISH: Game On!

And coming soon:

#6   SQUISH: Fear the Amoeba

Hi! I'm Squish—
I'm an amoeba.
I like Twinkies and comics.
And I'm not really pink,
I'm green.